The *Gift*

Your Call to Greatness

An Adult Faith Formation Program

Presented by
Christopher West

Student Workbook

ABBREVIATIONS

CCC   *Catechism of the Catholic Church*, Second Edition (Libreria Editrice Vaticana, 1997)

DC   *Deus Caritas Est*, Benedict XVI's encyclical letter *God is Love* (Pauline, 2006)

LF   *Letter to Families*, John Paul II's Letter to Families in the Year of the Family (Pauline, 1994)

LR   *Love and Responsibility*, Karol Wojtyla's philosophical work on human sexuality (Ignatius, 1993)

RH   *Redemptor Hominis*, John Paul II's encyclical letter on the Redeemer of Man (Pauline, 1979)

TOB   *Man and Woman He Created Them: A Theology of the Body*, John Paul II's general audience addresses on Human Love in the Divine Plan (Pauline, 2006)

WH   *Witness to Hope*, George Weigel's biography of Pope John Paul II (HarperCollins, 1999)

Nihil obstat: Rev. J. Brian Bransfield, S.T.D.
    Censor Librorum
    September 27, 2007

Imprimatur: +Justin Cardinal Rigali
    Archbishop of Philadelphia
    October 9, 2007

Published by Ascension Press
Post Office Box 1990
West Chester, PA 19380
Orders: 1-800-376-0520
www.AscensionPress.com

Cover design by Devin Schadt

Printed in the United States of America

ISBN 978-1-934217-32-0

CONTENTS

THERE IS A "GREAT MYSTERY"
CHISELED IN US –
A "CALL TO GREATNESS"
STAMPED IN OUR HUMANITY.
AND THIS CALL TO GREATNESS
IS A SHEER GIFT.
IT IS THE GIFT OF ALL GIFTS.

- In this talk, we are going to learn how to "read" this call to greatness that God has stamped in us so that we can open more fully to this gift and live it more abundantly.

- Why does John Paul II say we must "reconcile" ourselves to our own greatness? The reason is that we are often ready and willing to settle for something much *less* than what we are created for.

- The key to discovering our "greatness" is to get in touch with our deepest *desires*. If our desires often cause trouble for us, the problem is not that we desire *too much* – we desire *too little*.

1. DESIRE

A woman came to the well to draw water. She was *thirsty* (desire). Jesus said to her, "Everyone who drinks of this water will thirst again, but whoever drinks of the water that I shall give will never thirst again" (John 4:13-14).

- In this familiar story, Jesus approaches this woman's *physical desire* as a way to awaken her deeper *spiritual desire*.

- What does the human being desire? (Ask yourself: What do *I* desire?)

- All of our pursuits (security, peace, love, even temporal things such as money, food, and sexual union) have a common denominator. The human being is looking for "happiness," contentment, satisfaction, fulfillment.

- The question is this: What will bring the happiness we long for?

   1a. "We all want to live happily; in the whole human race there is no one who does not assent to this proposition, even before it is fully articulated" (St. Augustine, quoted in CCC 1718).

   1b. The "natural desire for happiness ... is of divine origin: God has placed it in the human heart in order to draw man to the One who alone can fulfill it" (CCC 1718).

The woman at the well is intrigued by Jesus' words, but she still doesn't understand: "Sir, give me this water, that I may no longer thirst, nor need to come back to this well to draw water" (see John 4:15).

- We are created for the *Infinite* and yearn for it. But we often seek to satisfy our yearning in *finite* things. When we do we "miss the mark."

- God gave us this world and its pleasures only as signs, "sacraments" or icons of the Infinite joys that await us in heaven. We must be careful not to turn these *icons* into *idols*. When we do we "miss the mark."

Jesus points the woman to her dearest "idol" – to the place where she has sought (unsuccessfully) to satisfy her deepest thirst – when he says, "Go, call your husband" (John 4:16).

- Jesus "knows everything about her" (see John 4:30). He knows that she has been sexually involved with several men (see John 4:18).

- Does Jesus condemn her for "missing the mark"? No! For he knows that, all along, *she was really looking for him* and the love he longs to give her:

"If you knew the gift of God, and who it is that is [speaking] to you … you would have asked him and he would have given you *living water*" (John 4:10). "Ask and you will receive, that your joy may be complete" (John 16:24).

> **1c.** "The man who wishes to understand himself thoroughly … must with his unrest, uncertainty and even his weakness and sinfulness, with his life and death, draw near to Christ. He must … enter into him with all his own self … in order to find himself. If that profound process takes place within him, he then bears fruit not only of adoration of God but also of deep wonder at himself. … In reality, the name for that deep amazement at man's worth and dignity [at man's greatness!] is the Gospel, that is to say: the Good News. It is also called Christianity" (RH 10).

2. Our Bodies: Sign of Our Greatness

"Theology of the Body"

In a series of 129 short talks delivered between 1979 and 1984, John Paul II helped the Church and the world to understand that man's "call to greatness" is *stamped right in his body* as male and female. Known as the "theology of the body" (TOB), these talks, according to papal biographer George Weigel, represent "one of the boldest reconfigurations of Catholic theology in centuries" (WH, p. 336).

- Since it offers an extensive biblical reflection on the meaning of marital love, the TOB is often reduced to a teaching on marriage. It is that, but it also *so much more*!

- It is critical to realize that *the TOB is not only for married people*. The TOB provides a lens through which to view and understand the very meaning of existence.

- The TOB is for the married, the divorced, the engaged, the single, the consecrated celibate, Christians, Jews, Muslims, atheists, farmers, doctors, lawyers, janitors, politicians, homemakers, children, teens, adults, the elderly – in short, theology of the *body* is for every*body*!

2a. Within the context of human sexuality and marital love, the TOB affords "the rediscovery of the meaning of the whole of existence, of the meaning of life" (TOB 46:6).

2b. Understanding the true meaning of the body and sexuality "concerns the whole Bible" (TOB 69:8). It plunges us into "the perspective of the whole Gospel, of the whole teaching, even more, of the whole mission of Christ" (TOB 49:3).

2c. The TOB "has barely begun to shape the Church's theology, preaching, and religious education. When it does, it will compel a dramatic development of thinking about virtually every major theme in the Creed" (WH, p. 853).

The Body Reveals God's Mystery

We cannot see God. As pure Spirit, God is totally beyond our vision. Yet, Christians believe that the invisible God has made himself visible. How?

2d. In "the body of Jesus 'we see our God made visible and so are caught up in love of the God we cannot see'" (CCC 477).

2e. "Through the fact that the Word of God became flesh, the body entered theology ... through the main door" (TOB 23:4).

God's mystery has been revealed *in human flesh* – "theology *of the body.*" This phrase is not only the title of a series of talks by John Paul II. It represents the very *logic* of Christianity.

2f. "The body, in fact, and only the body, is capable of making visible what is invisible: the spiritual and the divine. It has been created to transfer into the visible reality of the world the mystery hidden from eternity in God, and thus to be a sign of it" (TOB 19:4).

2g. Man "is a person in the unity of his body and his spirit. The body ... is a *spiritualized body*, just as man's spirit is ... *an embodied spirit*" (LF 19).

2h. "Should [man] aspire to be pure spirit and to reject the flesh as pertaining to his animal nature alone, then spirit and body would both lose their dignity. On the other hand, should he deny the spirit and consider matter, the body, as the only reality, he would likewise lose his greatness" (DC 5).

The Eternal Exchange of Love

What is the divine mystery that the body signifies?

- It is the mystery of Trinitarian Life and Love – of God's eternal *Communion* as Father, Son, and Holy Spirit.

- It is also the plan "hidden from eternity in God" (Ephesians 3:9) that man is destined in Christ to share in God's eternal bliss. *This* is our call to "greatness."

    2i. "God has revealed his innermost secret: God himself is an eternal exchange of love, Father, Son, and Holy Spirit, and he has destined us to share in that exchange" (CCC 221).

3. The Spousal Analogy

Scripture uses many images to describe God's love. Each has its own valuable place. But the spousal image is used far more than any other. It is also the favored image of the mystics.

- The Bible begins and ends with marriages – Adam-Eve and Christ-Church.

- The spousal "book ends" of Genesis and Revelation are a key for interpreting all that lies in between.

- We are *creatures* called to live in total (spousal) union with our *Creator.* This is the source of our "greatness" as human beings.

- The spousal analogy (like all analogies) is certainly limited and inadequate. No human image can do justice to the divine mystery. Yet JP II considers the spousal analogy the *least* inadequate.

God wanted this eternal plan of love and communion to be so obvious to us that he stamped an image of it in our very being by creating us as male and female.

    3a. Man *"became the image of God not only through his own humanity, but also through the communion of persons, which man and woman form from the very beginning ... On all this, right from the beginning, the blessing of fruitfulness descended"* (TOB 9:3).

"'For this reason a man shall leave his father and mother and be joined to his wife, and the two shall become one flesh.' This is a great mystery, and I mean in reference to Christ and the church" (Ephesians 5:21-32).

> **3b.** "The Church cannot therefore be understood ... unless we keep in mind the 'great mystery' ... expressed in the 'one flesh' [union] of marriage and the family" (LF 19).

> **3c.** "Saint Paul's magnificent synthesis concerning the 'great mystery' appears as the ... *summa*, in some sense, *of the teaching about God and man* which was brought to fulfillment by Christ" (LF 19).

4. THREE KEY WORDS OF CHRIST

In his discussions about the love of man and woman, Christ himself points to the marriage of the *beginning* and the Marriage of our ultimate *destiny*. Within *history* we live in a kind of "tension between these two poles" (TOB 71:2). This tension can awaken in us a great hope for the "redemption of our bodies" akin to the hope of a woman in labor (see Romans 8:22-23).

Our Origin

"For your hardness of heart Moses allowed you to divorce your wives, but from the beginning it was not so" (Matthew 19:8).

- We think all the tension, heartache, and difficulty in the male-female relationship is "normal." In the beginning it was not this way. Something has gone dreadfully wrong.

- The good news is that "Jesus came to restore creation to the purity of its origins" (CCC 2336).

"And the man and his wife were both naked, and were not ashamed" (Genesis 2:25).

- John Paul II calls this the "key" for understanding God's original plan for man and woman (see TOB 11:2).

- They experienced sexual desire (*eros*) only as the desire to love as God loves (*agape*). There is no shame (or fear) in love. "Perfect love casts out fear" (1 John 4:18).

Our History

"You have heard that it was said, 'You shall not commit adultery.' But I say to you that everyone who looks at a woman lustfully has already committed adultery with her in his heart" (Matthew 5:27-28).

4c. Should we *fear* the severity of Christ's words, or rather *have confidence* in their power to save us (see TOB 43:7)?

4d. "Why does Christ speak out in so forceful and demanding a way in the Sermon on the Mount? The answer is quite clear: … He wants to defend the full truth about the human person and his dignity" (LF 20).

4e. Christ's words are "an invitation to a pure way of looking at others, capable of respecting the spousal meaning of the body" (VS 15). Christ wants to inspire our sexual desires "with everything that is noble and beautiful," with "the supreme value which is love" (TOB 46:5).

In the Sermon on the Mount, Christ not only confirms the ethical demands of God's law, he proclaims the "new ethos" of the Gospel.

- *Ethos* refers to our inner-world of values, what attracts and repulses us.

- Christ doesn't want to impose laws on us. He wants to change our hearts – to "free us from the law" (see Galatians 5:18).

4f. "Christian ethos is characterized by *a transformation of the human person … such as to express and realize the value of the body and sex* according to the Creator's original plan" (TOB 45:3).

We "groan inwardly as we wait for … the redemption of our bodies" (Romans 8:23).

4g. The "redemption of the body" expresses itself not only in the resurrection as victory over death. It is present also in the words of Christ addressed to the men and women of history when he invites us to overcome lust even in the inner movements of our hearts (see TOB 86:6).

Our Destiny

"For in the resurrection they neither marry nor are given in marriage" (Matthew 22:30).

- Recall the two book-ends of the Bible. Which marriage is our ultimate fulfillment? The marriage of man and woman, or the marriage of Christ and the Church?

- Jesus is basically saying, "You no longer need a sign to point you *to* heaven when you are *in* heaven."

> **4h.** "Man's greatness and dignity consist in being ... called to live in intimate union with Christ" (John Paul II, speech of January 24, 1999).

> **4i.** In "the resurrection, we discover – in [a heavenly] perspective – the same ... 'spousal' meaning of the body ... in the encounter with the mystery of the living God ... face-to-face" (TOB 67:5).

> **4j.** "In the joys of their love [God gives spouses] here on earth a foretaste of the wedding feast of the Lamb" (CCC 1642).

> **4k.** The Church "longs to be united with Christ, her Bridegroom, in the glory of heaven" where she "will rejoice one day with [her] Beloved, in a happiness and rapture that can never end" (CCC 1821).

Some "have made themselves eunuchs for the sake of the kingdom of heaven" (Matthew 19:12).

- A eunuch is someone who cannot physically impregnate a woman.

- A eunuch "for the kingdom" is someone who freely forgoes sexual relations in order to devote all of his or her energies and desires to the union that alone can satisfy.

- Those who are celibate for the kingdom share in the same vocation to love as those who marry, but manifest this same vocation in a different manner.

> **4k.** On the basis of the same spousal meaning of the body there can be formed the love that commits a person to marriage for the whole of life (see Matthew 19:3-9), but there also can be formed the love that commits a person to a life of celibacy "for the kingdom" (see Matthew 19:11-12; see TOB 80:6). Celibacy for the kingdom has "acquired the meaning of an act of spousal love" (TOB 80:1).

5. The Language of the Body

"This is my commandment, that you love one another as I have loved you" (John 15:12). "'For this reason a man shall leave his father and mother and be joined to his wife, and the two shall become one flesh.' This is a great mystery, and I mean in reference to Christ and the church" (Ephesians 5:21-33).

- The body has a "language" that's meant to proclaim the truth of Christ's love. In this sense, John Paul II says that the body is "prophetic."

- He also points out that we must distinguish true from false prophets. If we can speak the truth with our bodies we can also speak lies.

   5a. One can speak of moral good and evil in the sexual relationship based on whether the couple gives to their union the character of a truthful sign (see TOB 37:6).

All questions of sexual morality, then, come down to this. Does this act truthfully image the love of Christ for the Church or does it not?

- Christ's love is *free*, *total*, *faithful*, and *fruitful*.

- This is precisely what spouses commit to at the altar, and what they are meant to express when they become "one flesh."

   5b. The language of the body has "clear cut meanings" (TOB 105:6) all of which are "'programmed' in a comprehensive way in conjugal consent" (TOB 106:3).

   5c. The "words themselves, 'I take you as my wife/as my husband' ... can only be fulfilled by conjugal intercourse." Here "we pass *to the reality* that corresponds to these words" (TOB 103:3).

   5d. "The true greatness of the human person is manifested in the fact that sexual activity is felt to require such a profound justification. It cannot be otherwise. *Man must reconcile himself to his natural greatness*" (LR, p. 236).

There is no possibility for true happiness in life unless we come to understand *who we are* as human beings – that is, unless we understand and fully embrace our "call to greatness."

- We are lied to at every turn in our culture about who we are, about what it means to be human, especially as concerns our bodies as male and female.

- If there is an enemy who wants to keep us from heaven, and if the union of man and woman is God's primary way of pointing us there, what do you think the enemy is going to attack?

6a. "This is the real drama: the modern means of social communication are ... falsifying the truth about man. Human beings are not the same thing as the images proposed by advertising and shown by the modern mass media. They are much more, in their physical and [spiritual] unity ... as persons. They are much more because of their vocation to love, which introduces them as male and female into the realm of the 'great mystery'" (LF 20).

6b. "The modern age has made great progress in understanding ... human psychology, but with regard to his deepest ... dimension contemporary man remains to a great extent a being unknown to himself. ... Such is the result of estrangement from that 'great mystery' [inscribed in our humanity]" (LF 19).

6c. "We are facing an immense threat to life: not only to the life of individuals but also to that of civilization itself" (LF 21). "Why is this happening? The reason is that our society has broken away from the full truth about ... what man and woman really are as persons. Thus it cannot adequately comprehend the real meaning of the gift of persons in marriage, responsible love at the service of fatherhood and motherhood, and the true grandeur of procreation" (LF 20)

6d. The TOB is "a kind of theological time bomb set to go off with dramatic consequences ... perhaps in the twenty-first century" (WH, 343).

I appeal to you: make it your mission in life to know and live the theology of *your* body. Take up a further study of the TOB. If we live this good news and share it with everyone we know, we shall not fall short of renewing the face of the earth.

Glossary

Communion of persons: Refers to the unity or "common union" established when persons mutually give and receive "the sincere gift of self." The male-female communion of persons in marriage is a created image of *the* Communion of Persons found in the Trinity.

Divine mystery: Refers to the two-fold "inner secret" of God: first, that God exists as a Trinity of persons in an eternal "exchange of love," and, second, that God has destined man (male and female) to participate in this exchange of love.

Embodied spirit: Refers to man as a person in the unity of his body and spirit.

Eros (Greek for sexual love) and *agape* (Greek for divine love): Christ's love is *free, total, faithful,* and *fruitful.* In Christian marriage, *eros* and *agape* are called to meet and bear fruit. If spouses are to be faithful to the "language of their bodies," sexual intercourse must express *agape.*

Ethic and *ethos*: An *ethic* is an objective moral law or command. *Ethos*, on the other hand, refers to the abiding inner desires of the heart—what attracts and repulses a person. In the Sermon on the Mount, Christ demonstrates that the ethic is not enough ("You have heard the command ... but I tell you ..."). Christ came to transform our *ethos*, i.e., to change our hearts.

Eunuch: Someone physically incapable of sexual intercourse. A *eunuch for the kingdom* is someone who chooses freely to forgo sexual intercourse in order to devote himself or herself totally to the "marriage of the Lamb" (i.e., the eternal union of Christ and the Church).

Gift of God: God's true disposition is one of self-donation ("gift").

Icon: In general, a sign or likeness that stands for an object by signifying or representing it. As it relates to the theology of the body, that which points us toward our ultimate destination of heaven.

Idol: An object or activity that is worshipped in place of God.

Incarnation: The doctrine that refers to the Eternal Word, the second Person of the Holy Trinity, taking on human flesh and being born of a woman.

Language of the body: Refers to the body's capacity to "speak" or "proclaim" God's love. It does so—or is meant to do so—most profoundly in the "one flesh" union of spouses. Here, spouses are meant to renew their marriage vows with their bodies.

Lust: Refers to sexual desire void of God's love. Lust leads a person toward *self-gratification* at the expense of the other, while love leads a person toward *self-donation* for the good of the other. Lust, therefore, is a *reduction* of the original fullness God intended for the sexual relationship.

Naked without shame (original nakedness): Adam and Eve were untainted by shame because they had no experience whatsoever of lust. Before sin, man and woman experienced sexual desire as the desire to love in God's image.

Purity of heart: To the degree that we are pure of heart we understand, see, and experience the body as God created it to be, as a revelation of his own divine mystery. "Blessed are the pure in heart, for they shall see God" (Matthew 5:8).

Redemption of the body: The restoration of the human person in his or her integrity as a unity of body and soul. It affords the recovery of God's original plan in the human heart. This redemption is not only something we hope for in the resurrection from the dead, it is already at work in us within history.

Resurrection of the body: The doctrine that the human body is also destined for everlasting life in union with the human soul. Eternal life is not only a "spiritual" reality. Man (male and female) is destined to share in the life of the Trinity as a body-person.

Sacrament: In its more ancient meaning, this refers to a physical sign that makes visible what is invisible. In its more strict meaning, sacrament refers to the seven signs of the new covenant (i.e., baptism, confirmation, Eucharist, penance, anointing of the sick, holy orders, and marriage) instituted by Christ to confer the grace of redemption.

Sacramentality of the body: Refers to the body's capacity of making visible what is invisible. The body proclaims a "great mystery"—the spiritual mystery of God's Trinitarian love and our call to share in that love through Christ.

Shame: In its negative sense, shame indicates that we have lost sight of the dignity and goodness of the body as a "theology"—a revelation of God's mystery. In its positive sense, shame indicates a desire to protect the goodness of the body from the degradation of lust.

Spiritualized body: Refers to the fact that the human body is "in breathed" not only with a spiritual soul but also, through the grace of redemption, with God's Holy Spirit.

Spousal analogy: The biblical use of marital love as an earthly image of God's love for Israel and, in the New Testament, Christ's love for the Church. Like all analogies, the spousal analogy is inadequate in communicating God's infinitely transcendent mystery. Yet, according to John Paul II, it is the most fitting human image of the divine mystery.

Spousal meaning of the body: The call to love as God loves inscribed in the human body as male and female. If we live according to the spousal meaning of our bodies, we fulfill the very meaning of our being and existence

Theology of the body: The study of how God reveals his mystery through the human body. This is also the title of John Paul II's 129 short talks on the subject.

About Christopher West

Christopher West is recognized around the globe for his work promoting an integral, biblical vision of human life, love, and sexuality. He serves as a research fellow and faculty member of the Theology of the Body Institute near Philadelphia, Pennsylvania. He has also lectured on a number of other prestigious faculties, offering graduate and undergraduate courses at St. John Vianney Seminary in Denver, the John Paul II Institute in Melbourne, Australia, and the Institute for Priestly Formation at Creighton University in Omaha.

Christopher is the best-selling author of several books and one of the most sought after speakers in the Church today. He and his wife, Wendy, live with their five children near Lancaster, Pennsylvania.

Other Resources by Christopher West

Books

Good News About Sex and Marriage: Answers to Your Honest Questions about Catholic Teaching (Servant, 2000; revised edition 2006)

Theology of the Body Explained: A Commentary on John Paul II's "Man and Woman He Created Them" (Pauline, 2003; revised edition, 2007)

Theology of the Body for Beginners: A Basic Introduction to John Paul II's Sexual Revolution (Ascension Press, 2004, revised edition 2009)

The Love That Satisfies: Reflections on Eros and Agape (Ascension Press, 2007)

Heaven's Song: Sexual Love as it was Meant to Be (Ascension Press, 2008)

Audio and Video Productions

Ascension Press is Christopher West's official publisher of audio and video presentations. For more information, visit AscensionPress.com or TheologyoftheBody.com or call 1-800-376-0520.

Speaking Engagements

To schedule a speaking engagement by Christopher West, visit ChristopherWest.com and click on the "speaking" link.